C.S.I.
DIAMOND ROBBERY

Darlene Stille

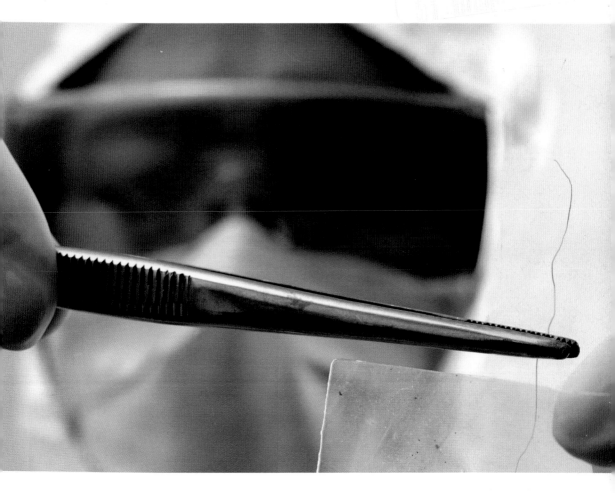

Copyright © ticktock Entertainment Ltd 2008

First published in Great Britain in 2008 by ticktock Media Ltd,
2 Orchard Business Centre, North Farm Road, Tunbridge Wells, Kent, TN2 3XF

ticktock project editor: Ruth Owen
ticktock project designer: Sara Greasley
ticktock picture researcher: Lizzie Knowles

**With thanks to series editors Honor Head and Jean Coppendale,
and consultant John Cassella, Principal Lecturer in Forensic Science, Staffordshire University, UK**

Thank you to Lorraine Petersen and the members of nasen

ISBN 978 1 84696 714 6 pbk

Printed in China

A CIP catalogue record for this book is available from the British Library.

Picture credits (t=top; b=bottom; c=centre; l=left; r=right):
age fotostock/ SuperStock: 12. Blend Images/ Jupiter Images: OFC, 4c. brandXpictures/ Jupiter Images: 29. Dr Tony
Brain/ Science Photo Library: 15r. Dr Jeremy Burgess/ Science Photo Library: 31t. Scott Camazine/ Alamy: 14-15c.
Michael Donne/ Science Photo Library: 26. Richard Dunkley/ Getty Images: 25. Mauro Fermariello/ Science Photo
Library: 1, 7t, 11. Steve Gschmeissner/ Science Photo Library: 8bl, 9, 13t, 13b. Mikael Karlsson/ Alamy: 22. Medical-
on-line/ Alamy: 8br. Phototake Inc./ Alamy: 14l. Science Photo Library: 2-3, 24t. Dr Jurgen Scriba/ Science Photo
Library: 18. Shutterstock: 4b, 5tl, 5tr, 8t x3, 10, 16, 17, 20-21, 23t, 24cl, 27b, 28 all. Andrew Syred/ Science Photo
Library: 19, 23b. Tek Images/ Science Photo Library: 5b, 6-7b. Tim Wright/ Corbis: 27t.

Every effort has been made to trace copyright holders, and we apologise in advance for any omissions. We would be
pleased to insert the appropriate acknowledgments in any subsequent edition of this publication.

Contents

CHAPTER 1

DIAMOND ROBBERY!

There has been a robbery at a jewellery shop.

The robber stole diamond rings from the shop's safe.

Safe

The diamond rings are worth one million pounds.

The robber cut the wires to the burglar alarm.
The robber smashed the shop's CCTV cameras.

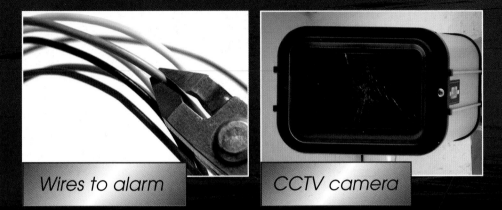

Wires to alarm

CCTV camera

No one saw the robbery happen.
At first, it seems there are no clues at the crime scene.

The police call for the crime scene investigators (CSIs).

Crime scene
investigator

The CSIs know that criminals always leave clues. It may be
a hair, or a tiny piece of their clothing, called a fibre.

**These little clues are called
trace evidence.**

CHAPTER 2

LOOKING FOR TRACES

Crime scene investigators search a crime scene for fingerprints, hairs and fibres.

The CSIs wear gloves, masks, shoe covers and white overalls. The gloves stop the CSIs from leaving their own fingerprints at the crime scene. The overalls stop the CSIs from dropping hairs at the crime scene, or fibres from their own clothing.

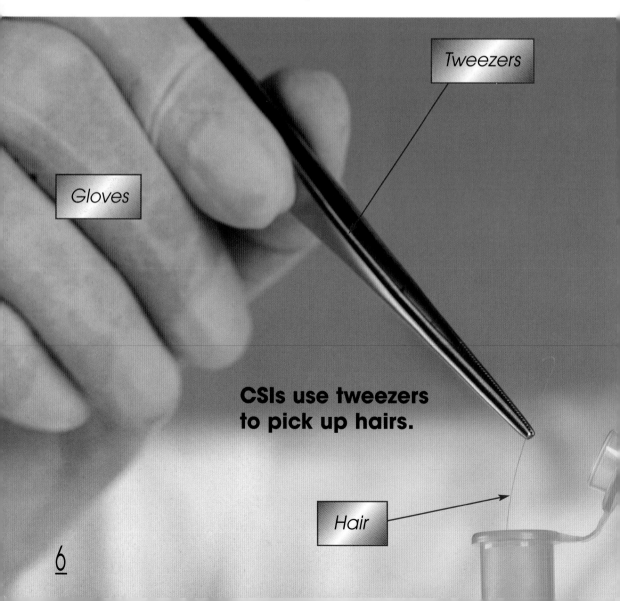

Tweezers

Gloves

CSIs use tweezers to pick up hairs.

Hair

They use a special vacuum cleaner to clean floors and surfaces at a crime scene.

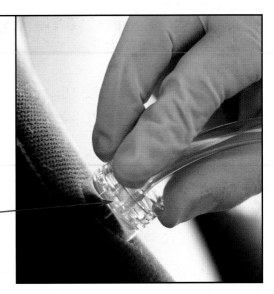

Vacuum cleaner

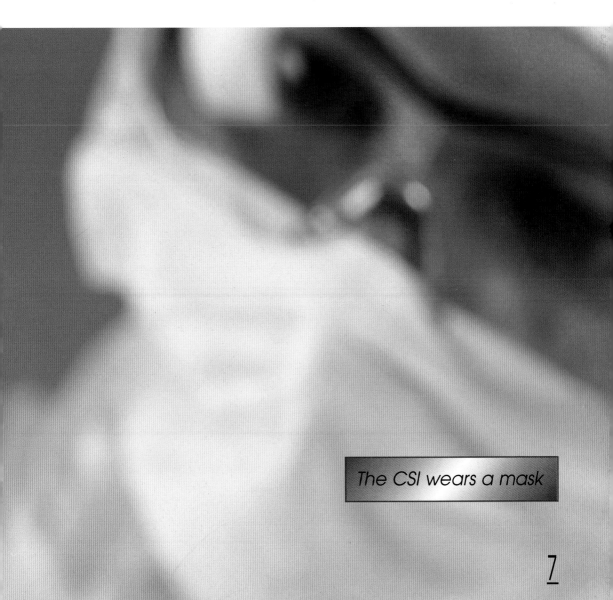

The CSI wears a mask

Hair at a crime scene can fall from any part of the criminal's body.

Different types of hair grow on the face, arms and legs.

Old hairs fall out as new hairs grow.
About 100 hairs fall out of your head every day.

Hair can also come from a criminal's clothing, from a pet or from a fur coat.

All hairs look different under a microscope.

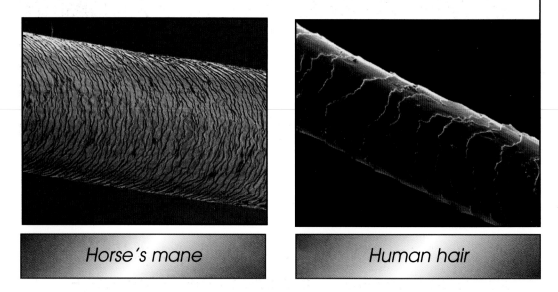

Horse's mane *Human hair*

Sometimes hairs can get pulled out in a struggle or by accident.

A part of the hair, called the follicle, is in the skin.
When a hair is pulled out, the follicle stretches.

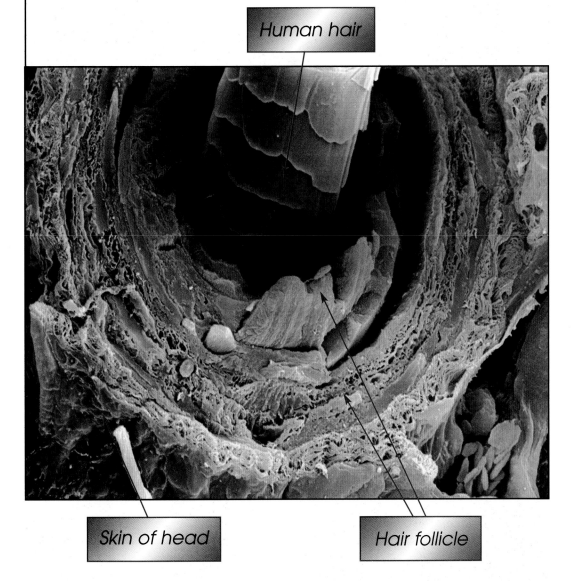

Human hair

Skin of head

Hair follicle

If CSIs find several hairs with stretched follicles, this
could mean there was a struggle at the crime scene.

The CSIs find no fingerprints at the jewellery shop. The robber must have worn gloves.

They find no fibres.

But they do find some hairs, and one very interesting clue...

...a short, white hair.

The trace evidence is put in special plastic evidence bags.

CSIs at a crime scene must be very careful. One piece of evidence cannot touch another. Different pieces of evidence are put in separate bags. Each evidence bag is labelled.

Label

Evidence bag

NEED TO KNOW

If the police have a suspect, they can collect hairs from that person. The suspect's hair, and a hair from the crime scene might match.

CHAPTER 3   AT THE LAB

The evidence bags and the vacuum cleaner bag are taken to the crime lab.

A forensic scientist examines the hairs under a powerful microscope.

Forensic scientist

Microscope

First, she checks to find out if the hairs are from an animal or a human.

If a hair is human, the forensic scientist checks if it's rough, smooth, straight or curly. This tells the scientist what part of the body the hair came from. It can also tell the scientist what race the person is.

Scales

Blond human hair from a white person

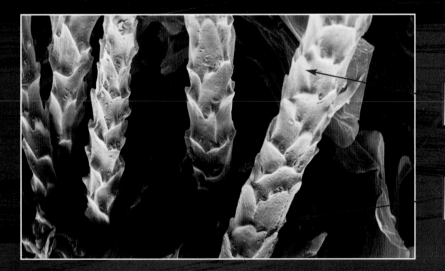

Scales

Skin

Dog hairs

NEED TO KNOW
Hairs are covered in scales. They overlap like tiles on a roof. Forensic scientists can use scale patterns to tell human and animal hairs apart.

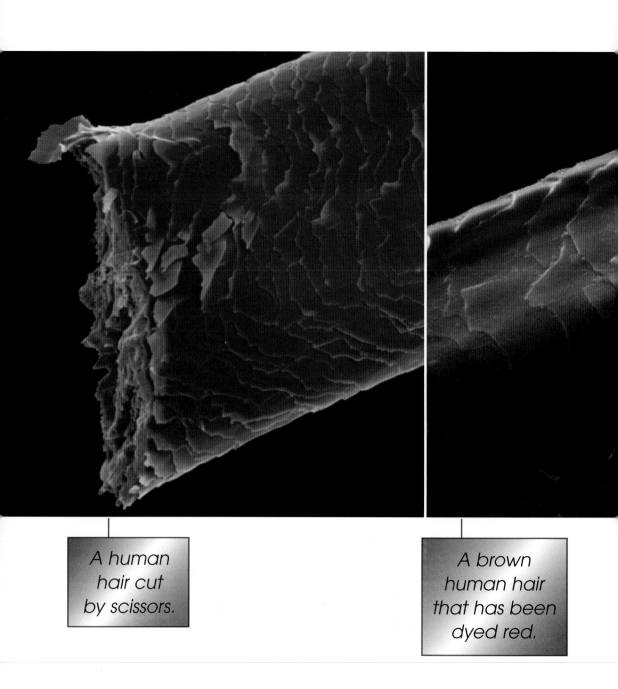

A human
hair cut
by scissors.

A brown
human hair
that has been
dyed red.

**Hairs can give forensic scientists
clues to a suspect's hairstyle.**

A permed hair. The scales have been stripped away by the perm chemicals.

They can tell if a hair was cut by scissors or a razor.

If CSIs find a human hair at a crime scene, the forensic scientists can do a DNA test.

Cells in our body and hair are unique.
They contain unique information called DNA.

Identical twins

Only identical twins have the same DNA.

A DNA test can be done on a single hair.

Special machines read the DNA.

They show the information in a pattern called a profile.

DNA profile

Police databases store DNA profiles. The profiles
are from people who have been arrested for a
crime in the past.

Sometimes the police can match a DNA profile from a
hair at a crime scene to a DNA profile on their database.

This leads them to a suspect.

Forensic scientists can test hair to find out if a person was taking drugs.

When a person uses drugs, chemicals stay in a fixed position in their hair. Each hair acts like a timeline showing when the person took drugs.

Hair sample

Section for testing

A hair sample can be cut into sections. Hair from close to the head will only be weeks old. Hair from further down the sample will be months old. The hair sections can be matched to time periods and tested for drugs.

Cat hair

The hairs found
at the jewellery
shop all belong to
the shop's workers.

Except for the short,
white hair.

It is not a human hair!

RESULT
The white hair is from a
white cat. No one at the shop
owns a cat. Did the hair come from
the robber's cat?

CHAPTER 4

A COLD CASE HEATS UP!

**The police are at a deadend.
But then there is a breakthrough!**

There is a robbery at another jewellery shop.

A witness sees a car speeding from the crime scene. The witness writes down the car's licence plate number.

The CSIs search the new crime scene.

They find more white hairs.
They also find fibres on a door handle.
Did the robber catch his or her clothes
on the door handle?

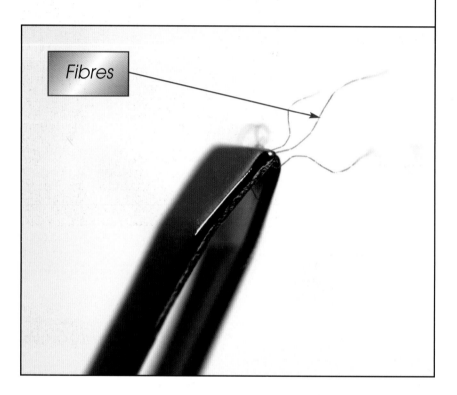

Fibres

Fibres at a crime scene can come from clothes,
towels or sheets, and carpets or curtains.

Fibres from a carpet can stick to hair on a body.
Fibres from a sweater can stick to a chair.

Back at the lab, the forensic scientists want to know if the fibres are natural or man-made.

Natural fibres come from plants or animals.

Wool fibres come from sheep and other animals with woolly coats.

Cotton fibres come from cotton plants.

Cotton plant

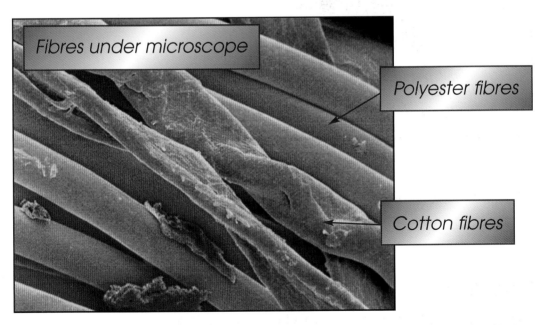

Fibres under microscope

Polyester fibres

Cotton fibres

Man-made fibres such as nylon and polyester are made from chemicals.

The forensic scientists examine the fibres from the jewellery shop under a microscope.

Angora wool fibres

Angora goat

RESULT
The fibres are natural.
They are blue angora wool.
This type of wool comes
from angora goats.

None of the jewellery shop workers own a blue angora sweater.

Could it belong to the robber?

The wool fibres are dyed blue.

Dyes can be made from plants, but most modern dyes are made from chemicals.

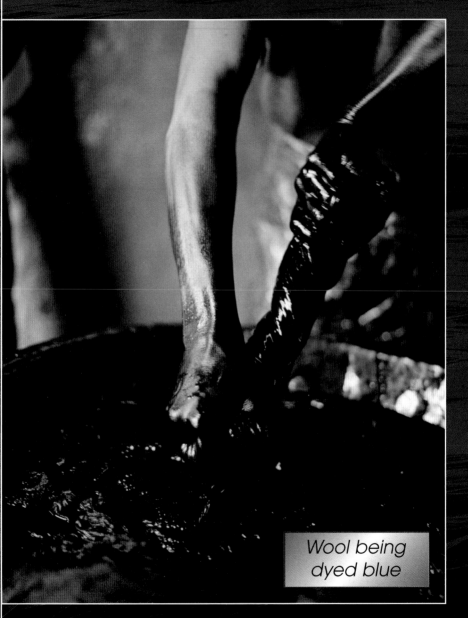

Wool being dyed blue

Every batch of dye is a little bit different. Factories label and keep records of each batch of dye that they make.

CHAPTER 5

BUILDING A CASE

The police track the car licence plate from the second robbery. They visit the car's owner.

The police search the car owner's house.
They find a blue angora wool sweater.

But they find no signs of a white cat.

Sticky tape

CSIs search the car.
They use sticky tape
to lift some fibres
from the car.

RESULT
The fibres match the carpet
at the second jewellery shop.
The car owner is now
a suspect.

The police track down the factory that made the dye and the blue angora sweater.

The factory owner tells the police that she used the dye to make just 100 blue angora sweaters.

The police go to see the suspect again.

A white cat jumps the fence from next door. It goes into the suspect's house.

RESULT
The neighbour's cat is a match for the white hair found at the crime scene.

CHAPTER 6

THE TRIAL

The police charge the suspect with the robbery.

In court, he says he is innocent!

THE PROSECUTION

- The suspect's car was seen at the crime scene.

- Carpet fibres from the jewellery shop were in the car.

- The suspect owns a rare blue angora sweater.

- The suspect's neighbour owns a white cat.

THE DEFENCE

- The suspect says he picked up the carpet fibres when he shopped at the jewellery shop.

- He says his car was in a car park on the night of the robbery. Someone took his car then put it back.

- The defence lawyer says the hair and fibre evidence is not strong enough to convict the suspect.

Jury

Suppose you are on the jury.

Would you vote

GUILTY OR NOT GUILTY?

NEED TO KNOW WORDS

CCTV camera Closed-circuit Television Camera. It records what is happening and sends it to a TV screen where it can be watched or recorded.

crime lab A laboratory with equipment that is used for scientific experiments and tests on crime scene evidence.

crime scene Any place where a crime has happened.

crime scene investigator (CSI) A person who examines crime scenes and collects evidence.

defence The lawyer, or group of lawyers, who try to prove in court that a person accused of a crime is innocent.

DNA The special code in the centre (or nucleus) of each person's cells. Our DNA makes us all unique.

evidence Facts and signs that can show what happened during a crime.

forensic scientist An expert who gathers detailed information from a crime scene and analyses it to work out what happened.

jury A group of people in a court who listen to all the evidence. Then they decide if the accused is innocent or guilty.

lawyer An expert in the law who is hired to speak in court and give people advice about the law.

prosecution The lawyer, or group of lawyers, who try to prove in court that a person accused of a crime is guilty.

race A group of people with the same skin colour, or culture or ancestors.

suspect A person who is thought to have committed a crime.

trace A very small mark, sign or substance that is left behind.

unique The only one of its kind.

witness Someone who saw a crime being committed or who has information about a crime.

NEED TO KNOW FACTS

- **Inside a hair**

  A hair has an outer layer called the cuticle. This is made of colourless scales that overlap each other. The cortex is the inner part of the hair. The cortex is important to forensic scientists because this is the part that gives hair its colour.

- **Haircut evidence**

  Forensic scientists can sometimes work out when someone last had a haircut. A newly cut hair is square cut. After three weeks, the hair tip begins to look rounded.

- **Time to shampoo**

  A forensic scientist can tell if you've washed your hair or not. The black spots on the hairs below are four-day-old dirt!

CRIME ONLINE

Websites

http://www.fbi.gov/page2/july07/trace070207.htm
How the FBI used hair and fibre evidence to solve a crime

http://www.fbi.gov/kids/6th12th/6th12th.htm
How the FBI investigates crimes

http://www.howstuffworks.com/csi5.htm
All about the world of CSI

www.sciencenewsforkids.org/articles/20041215/wordfind.asp
A science site that includes a crime lab wordsearch

INDEX